A TEMPLAR BOOK

First published in the UK in 2015 by Templar Publishing.
This edition published in the UK in 2017 by Templar Publishing,
an imprint of Kings Road Publishing, part of the Bonnier Publishing Group,
The Plaza, 535 King's Road, London, SW10 0SZ
www.templarco.co.uk
www.bonnierpublishing.com

ISBN 978-1-78370-849-9

Illustrated by Sarah Horne
Written by Emma Dodson & Tasha Percy
Designed by Jenny Hilborne and Mark Mckinley
Edited by Eryl Nash and Tasha Percy

Printed in China

templar
books

THE REALLY Gross BODY BOOK

Emma Dodson & Sarah Horne

Welcome to your really GROSS body!

You might have noticed that your body can be a bit gross! But even the most revolting bits have a purpose. Read on to find out more...

EAR WAX

SWE

Sweat
the bod
natura
cooling
system, but
why is it
so stinky?

FARTS

Ever wanted to know why quiet farts are always the most smelly? Have you heard about the French performer who found fame through farting?

BUM

POOP

The longest poo ever recorded was 7.9 metres long! What do you think your poo says about you...?

What is SNOT?

Snot is the slimy, sticky, slippery stuff that hangs around in (and occasionally drips out of) your nose. Its posh name is *mucus*.

WHAT'S THE POINT OF SNOT?

Snot traps all the germs, dust, dirt and pollen that goes up your nostrils each time you breathe in. Your brilliant bogeys stop this stuff from making you ill.

surf's up!

SNEEZING IS GOOD FOR YOU... BUT NOT FOR THOSE STANDING NEXT TO YOU!

Sneezing helps keep your nose clean. When you sneeze, all the nasty germs trapped in your nose shoot out with a load of snot.

A sneeze can travel at about 65 kilometres per hour, sending germs far and wide, so make sure you always ATISHOO into a tissue!

SNOT-ORRIFIC!

The longest sneezing fit ever recorded lasted 978 days!

A-TISHOO!

Iguanas are thought to sneeze more than any other animal. Sneezing is their way of getting rid of unwanted salts.

SNOT Funny!

There are many types of snot in your nose and they come in a lot of different colours and shapes.

FOUL FACT

Humans aren't the only animals who pick their noses... many monkeys do it as well!

DID YOU KNOW?

The official word for picking your nose is rhinotillexomania!

IT'S SNOT A SNACK!

Bogeys can be green, brown, squishy or crusty. They are dried-up bits of snot that are full of dirt and germs. Despite this, some people think of their bogeys as handy snacks!

WHY IS SNOT GREEN?

If you take a close look at your snot, you will see that it is not always green...

...in fact, depending on your health and what you've been breathing in, your snot can come in a range of different colours. For example your snot will be white if you've eaten a lot of dairy or black if you have been sniffing dirt or dust.

What is VOMIT?

Vomiting is the body's way of getting germs or rotten food out of the stomach.

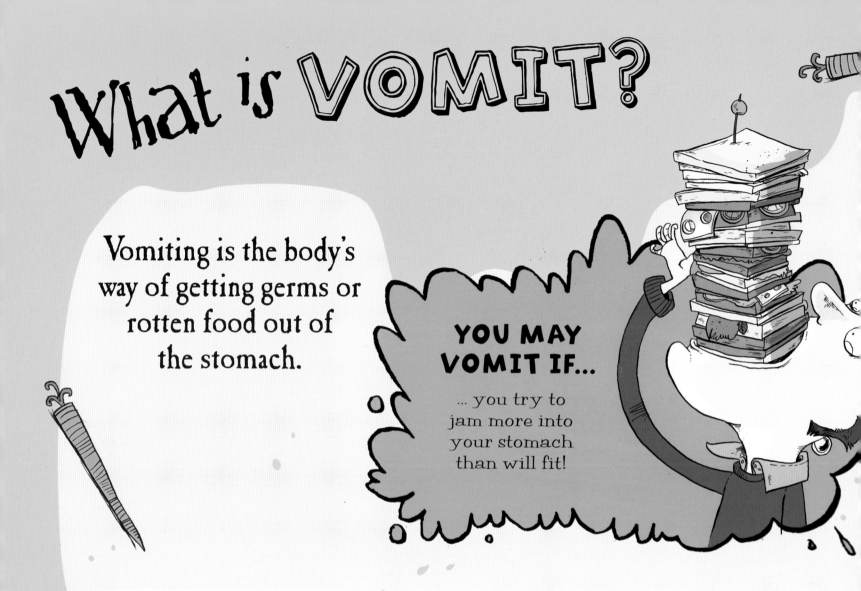

YOU MAY VOMIT IF...

... you try to jam more into your stomach than will fit!

WHEN YOU VOMIT...

Your stomach muscles will start to squeeze the contents of your stomach.

Your mouth produces lots of saliva to protect your mouth from fierce stomach acids.

Half-digested food and acids travel up your throat and comes shooting out of your mouth.

A SICK IDENTIFICATION!

Traces of human DNA left behind at a crime scene can be used to catch criminals. A nervous Australian robber, Ahmed Habib Jalloul, was sick on the job and got caught out by the DNA in his own vomit!

SICK BAG

Find out inside:
- What's in your vomit?

- Why are there always carrots in your vomit?

Vomit is soggy half-digested food mixed with slimy stomach mucus, saliva, smelly stomach acids and other chemicals that help your food digest.

WHY ARE THERE ALWAYS CARROTS IN MY VOMIT?

Generally it is not carrot pieces that are found in vomit but small pieces of stomach lining. Sometimes vomit comes out a greenish colour. This is because it contains green stuff called bile, which digests foods.

Super SICK

Different things can make people vomit. Did you know there was a boy who was sick as a form of entertainment?

DID YOU KNOW?

If you try to stop yourself from throwing up by closing your mouth, the vomit will just shoot out of your nose!

VOMITING FROGS

In 1694 Theodorus Döderlein's party trick was to swallow small animals and then vomit them up. His best was 162 woodlice, 32 caterpillars, 21 newts, 4 frogs, some toads, 4 millipedes, 2 worms, 2 butterflies, 2 ants and 1 beetle. The prankster stopped when his doctors made him drink horse urine to kill the animals 'living in his stomach'.

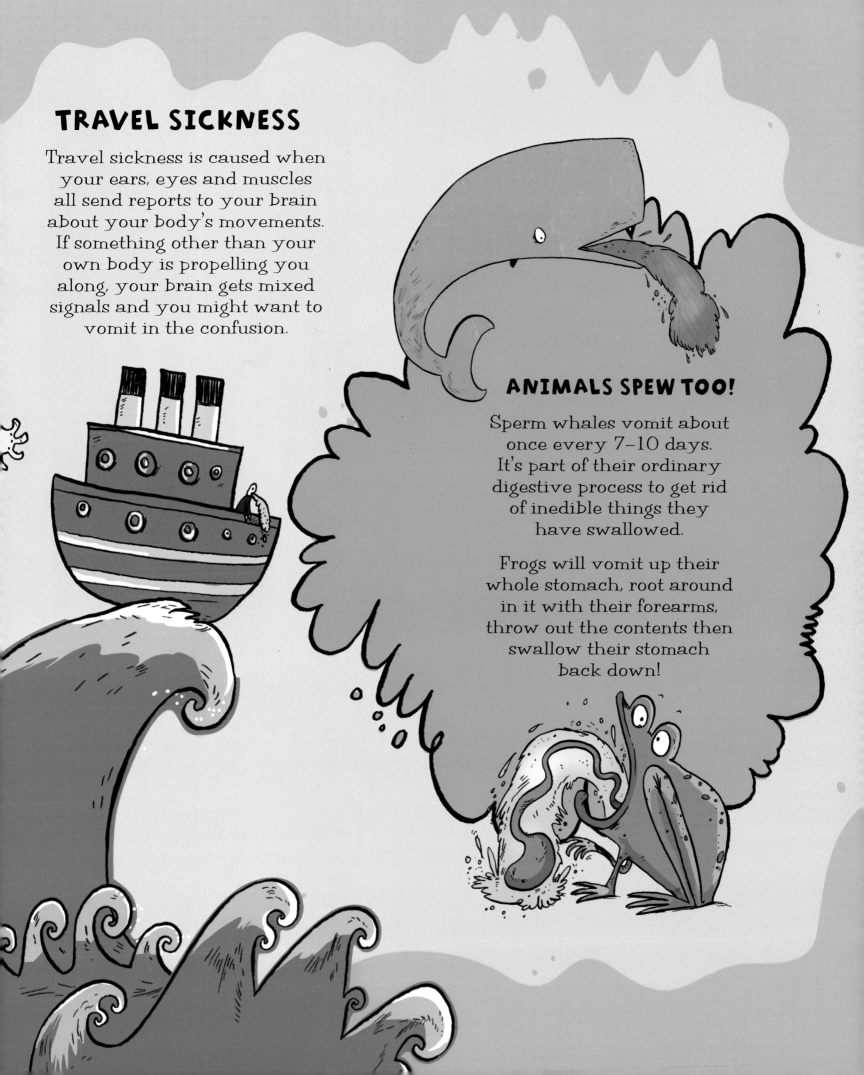

TRAVEL SICKNESS

Travel sickness is caused when your ears, eyes and muscles all send reports to your brain about your body's movements. If something other than your own body is propelling you along, your brain gets mixed signals and you might want to vomit in the confusion.

ANIMALS SPEW TOO!

Sperm whales vomit about once every 7–10 days. It's part of their ordinary digestive process to get rid of inedible things they have swallowed.

Frogs will vomit up their whole stomach, root around in it with their forearms, throw out the contents then swallow their stomach back down!

Fantastic FARTS!

Flatulence (the fancy word for farting) is when a mixture of gases escape through the bum.

So where do these gases come from? Everyone swallows a bit of air while eating or drinking. The rest of the gas is made in your intestines as your food is digested.

WHAT'S IN A FART?

- 21% Hydrogen
- 9% Carbon dioxide
- 7% Methane
- 3% Oxygen
- 59% Nitrogen
- 1% Other

DID YOU KNOW?

An average person will fart approximately 14 times per day!

Le Pétomane French Fartiste!

In the late 1800s, a French performer became famous for his strange talents.

By firing air from his bum, he could blow out candels, fart well-known tunes and propel jets of water across big distances.

SILENT BUT DEADLY!

The gas we swallow with our food is non-smelly and we fart it out in fairly large, noisy bubbles. PARP! But the stinky gas produced in our guts is farted out in much smaller amounts that don't make much noise.

THE WORLD'S TOP TEN FARTERS

It's not just humans that fart — animals do too, but some more than others! Here's a run-down of the biggest farters...

1. TERMITES
2. CAMELS
3. ZEBRAS
4. SHEEP
5. COWS
6. ELEPHANTS
7. LABRADORS
8. HUMANS (vegetarians)
9. HUMANS (non-vegetarians)
10. GERBILS

Termites chomp through so much wood that a huge amount of gas is produced in their guts. In total, termite farts produce more methane than all of our cars, planes and factories put together!

Beans contain sugars that your stomach can't easily digest. When the beans arrive in your large intestine, the bacteria there break down these sugars. In the process they produce a lot of gas!

BAKED
BEANS

PUT A PLUG IN IT...

Scientists in New Zealand are cutting the amount of methane burped and farted into the atmosphere by changing the diets of their sheep and giving fart-fighting injections!

FART-FREE ZONE!

Special SPIT

Saliva (or spit) is what helps us taste, eat and swallow food.

PURRSIL

REMOVES 99.9% OF ALL KNOWN STAINS FROM YOUR CAT

DOGGY DRIBBLE

Have you ever noticed how dogs always pant when they're hot? That's because they sweat through their mouths! Eurgh!

Cat saliva contains a natural soap-like substance that helps keep cats' fur clean. But it also contains bacteria – so it's not quite as hygienic for humans!

SPIT FACT

The average person will produce enough spit in a day to fill a large drinks bottle!

WHAT'S THE POINT OF SPIT?

Saliva is produced by salivary glands in the mouth.

When we see, smell and even think about food, our salivary glands get very excited and start churning out loads of spit.

These enzymes also help clean bacteria out of the mouth and fight any infections.

Spit is mostly made up of water and its main job is to mix up with the food we put in our mouths, and then help it slip down easily into the stomach.

Special enzymes in the saliva also begin to break down the food and make it easier to digest.

ACID ATTACK!

Human saliva can help to keep acid levels under control. If acids are allowed to build up too much they begin to eat away at your teeth!

yum.

Sweet SWEAT

Sweat is how moisture leaves the body through the skin.

SMELLY SOCKS!

There are 250,000 sweat glands in your feet. No wonder those socks smell so bad!

DID YOU KNOW?

A vegetarian's sweat can smell sweeter than that of a meat-eater!

SWEATING IS GOOD FOR YOU

Sweating is the body's natural cooling system. When you get hot, you sweat and as the sweat leaves your skin, it cools you down.

It can also help to remove toxins from the body and boost the immune system.

SWEAT

Sweat is mostly made up of water, with some salt and a small amount of other minerals.

STINKY PITS

In the hairiest parts of the body, the apocrine glands produce sweat that can become really, really stinky! Sweat from these glands attracts the bacteria that cause the smell.

SWEAT'S NOT SO BAD

Sweat alone doesn't smell too bad. The nasty smell is the bacteria that breaks down the sweat combined with the sweat.

Lots of POO

Poo is how leftover food, worn out blood cells, germs and other bits of unwanted rubbish leave your body.

GOOD POO OR BAD POO?

There are many different types of poo. From hard and lumpy to smelly and runny, see how your poo measures up!

CRACKED KAK

Although not a perfect poo, these sausage-shaped poos with cracked surfaces do suggest everything is functioning well!

BEAUTIFUL BANANA

This is a good poo to do! A soft poo that is banana-shaped means you are healthy and have a balanced diet.

PEBBLE POO

These are small, round, hard lumps that are difficult to get out. They might mean you haven't been drinking enough water or eating enough fruit and veg.

LUMPY LOG

These are sausage-shaped but lumpy and bumpy. They're a bit healthier than pebble poos but still mean you need to drink more water and eat more healthily.

SLIPPY SPLASHER

When you're ill, your large intestine sometimes can't suck the water out of your food quite fast enough—so it all comes out with your poo. This is diarrhoea!

MUSHY MUD-BUNNIES

Soft, mushy poo can mean you have too much fibre in your diet or that you're ill.

CHUNKY LOAF

Some foods, like carrots and sweetcorn, are tricky to digest and might come out looking just like they did when they went in! Try chewing your food a bit more before you swallow.

STINKY FACT

The longest poo ever recorded was 7.9 metres long! The record-holder ate a high-fibre diet and didn't go to the toilet for a whole week before the giant dump...

POOING: A JOURNEY

WHAT IS POO?

About 75% of your poo is made of water (how very boring!). The rest is made up of waste matter from the body, including any food you cannot digest, dead cells and bacteria.

1. Food goes into the mouth and is chewed up. This is called mastication.

2. Mashed-up food is swallowed and travels down your throat to your stomach.

3. In the stomach, digestive juices and bile break down the food.

4. Food that cannot be digested travels through the large intestine and out of your bum.

DID YOU KNOW?

A human will poop out between 10 and 50 tons in a lifetime!

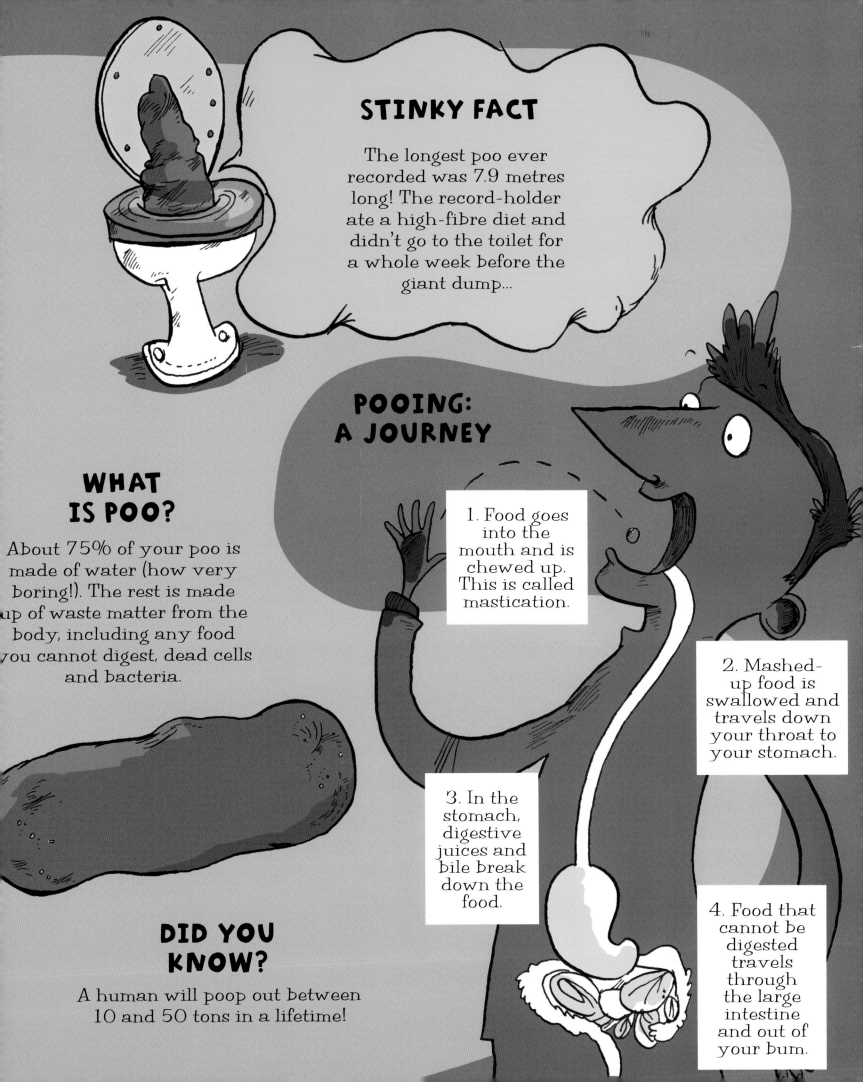

DO DO

Poo can be changed by what you eat and some can even be found in space.

HOT POO

How come after a spicy curry your bottom can feel the after-effects? The chemical in chilli that causes a burning feeling in your mouth is called capsaicin. This can irritate the digestive system, causing poo to be rushed out of your body as diarrhoea...

DUNG BEETLE

Dung beetles feed on poo! Some dung beetles live in poo, while others make balls of poo and roll it along with them.

COSMIC POOP

When the Apollo astronauts set off home after landing on the Moon, they left behind anything they wouldn't need... including Defecation Collection Devices – bags of poo! What must it be like now, more than 40 years later?

MAGIC MUSCLES

Two ring-like sphincter muscles hold your poo in until you're ready to go. The inner ring keeps your bottom closed until you need to poo. You can clench the outer ring for extra protection – just in case you need to sneeze at the wrong moment! Oops!

FLOATERS

Poos that float are known as 'floaters' – they're made when the gases made by the bacteria in your gut haven't formed farts but have stayed in the poo, making it all foamy.

BLOOD and SCABS!

When you cut or graze yourself, scabs are what keep germs from getting into the wound and stop your blood from pouring out!

BLUE BLOOD

Your blood is red because it contains a bright red protein called haemoglobin. Crabs, however, have blue blood (as it contains copper, which turns it blue!)

VAMPIRE BATS

Vampire bats have chemicals in their spit that prevent scabs from forming. This helps them suck blood out of their victims more easily.

DID YOU KNOW?

The average human adult has approximately 5 litres of blood in their body.

BUSY BLOOD

Blood is made up of around 55% plasma, which is mostly water and important cells that protect you against germs and diseases.

Blood cells also carry oxygen and essential nutrients to all the corners of your body and carry waste products, such as carbon dioxide, away.

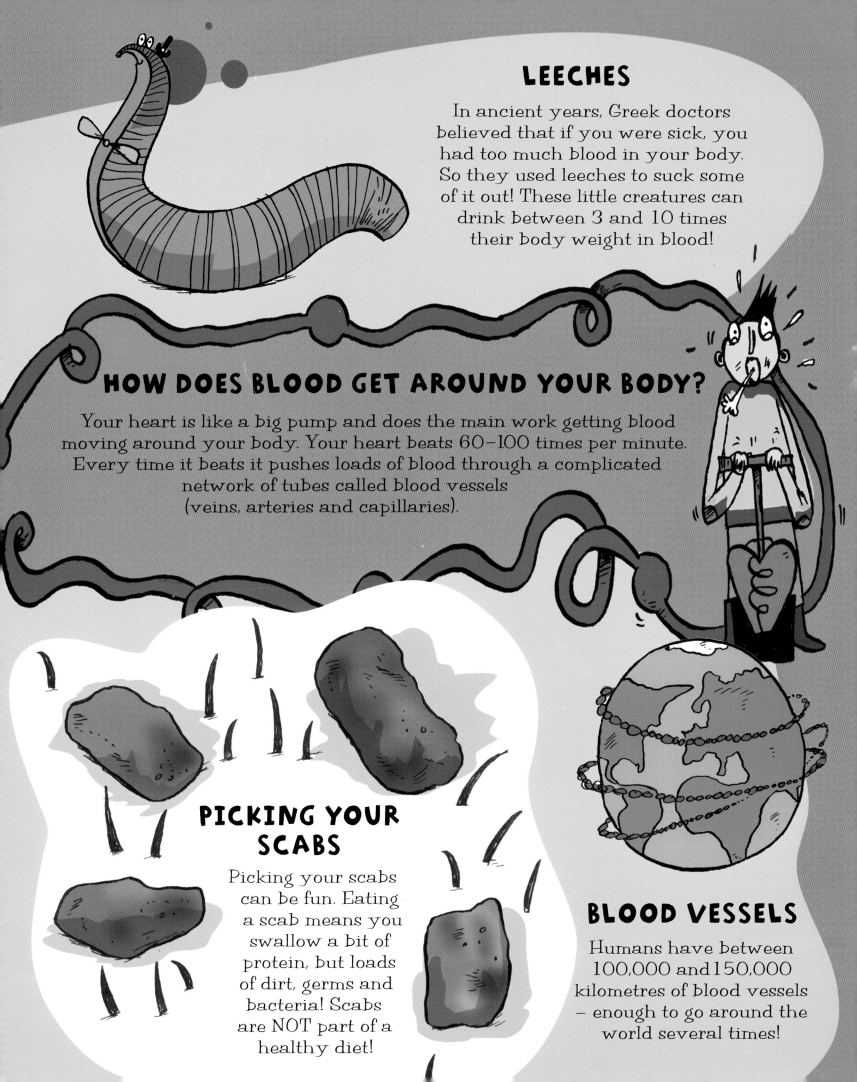

LEECHES

In ancient years, Greek doctors believed that if you were sick, you had too much blood in your body. So they used leeches to suck some of it out! These little creatures can drink between 3 and 10 times their body weight in blood!

HOW DOES BLOOD GET AROUND YOUR BODY?

Your heart is like a big pump and does the main work getting blood moving around your body. Your heart beats 60–100 times per minute. Every time it beats it pushes loads of blood through a complicated network of tubes called blood vessels (veins, arteries and capillaries).

PICKING YOUR SCABS

Picking your scabs can be fun. Eating a scab means you swallow a bit of protein, but loads of dirt, germs and bacteria! Scabs are NOT part of a healthy diet!

BLOOD VESSELS

Humans have between 100,000 and 150,000 kilometres of blood vessels – enough to go around the world several times!

Wee, pee and PIDDLE!

Your body takes in toxins from everything you eat, drink and even breathe in. Urinating is a way to push these toxins out of your body.

WHAT DOES THIS COLOUR MEAN?

Red, brown or blue = cause for concern!

Green = eating a lot of vitamin B.

Pink = eating beetroot.

Orange = drinking carrot juice.

Dark yellow = dehydrated.

Pale yellow = healthy!

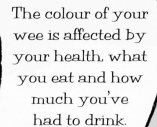

The colour of your wee is affected by your health, what you eat and how much you've had to drink.

DID YOU KNOW?

Ancient Roman spies used urine as invisible ink to write secrets between the lines of their official documents. The messages only appeared when heated...

USING YOUR LOAF

Before they discovered yeast, European bakers used urine to help their bread rise... tasty!

LAKE PIDDLE

a lifetime, the kidneys clean more than 1 million gallons of water – enough to fill a small lake!

STRANGE MOUTHWASH

In some cultures, pee has been used as mouthwash – thought to make the teeth super sparkling white.

LOBSTERS AT LOGGERHEADS

Male lobsters have bladders in their heads and when they fight they squirt each other in the face with wee!

WHAT'S IN YOUR WEE?

Urine is 95% water. The other 5% is made up of bits of dissolved waste from the bloodstream,

an assortment of salts and chemicals, some proteins and a few hormones.

TOILETRIES

In the past, ladies of England and France would use pee to give their skin a fresh glow. They would either pee in their hands to soften them or use puppy pee!